EVENING SUNSET, CLOSE OF DAY

Marcia De'Winter

MINERVA PRESS
LONDON
ATLANTA MONTREUX SYDNEY

EVENING SUNSET, CLOSE OF DAY
Copyright © Marcia De'Winter 1998

All Rights Reserved

No part of this book may be reproduced in any form
by photocopying or by any electronic or mechanical means,
including information storage or retrieval systems,
without permission in writing from both the copyright
owner and the publisher of this book.

ISBN 0 75410 261 0

First Published 1998 by
MINERVA PRESS
195 Knightsbridge
London SW7 1RE

NORTH EASTERN LIBRARY SERVICE AREA LIBRARY, DEMESNE AVE BALLYMENA CO. ANTRIM BT43 7BG	
8000867 4	
FARR	25/05/99
821.914	£3.99
CBK	

Printed in Great Britain for Minerva Press

EVENING SUNSET, CLOSE OF DAY

Contents

Evening Sunset, Close of Day	7
Nights of Silence	8
Clothe Me In Light	9
Snowdrop	10
Wasted Years	11
Sands and Horizons	13
Seasons	14
Reclusive Mind	15
Eyes of a Child	16
When Jesus Called	18
Spirits High and Low	20
No Bed of Roses	21
Memories and Daydreams	22
The Beggar	23
Face of an Angel	24
The Vagabond	25
Out on a Wing	26
Where Angels Go To Sleep	27
Time Does Not Wait	29
Wasting Time	30

Selfish Ambition	31
Meadows Soft and Green	32
In Memories of Sleep	33
Gifts of Love	34
Creations	35
Days and Dreams Gone By	36
The Gambler	37
Deep Rivers, High Mountains	38
Simplicity of Life	39
Angels from Above	40
The Coming of Spring	42
Blood Really Counts	44
Peace in our Green and Pleasant Land	46
Mechanical Inventions	48
Autumn Leaves	50
Sarcasm and Wit	51
Inspirations	52
The Wanderer	53
Stolen Jewel	54
Princess in Heaven	55

Evening Sunset, Close of Day

To stroll in the shadow of dusky light,
Red skies above, a wonderful sight.
Shepherds in watching all quiet alone,
Afraid of no warning or gentle atone.
Warm breeze of summer fading away,
Rabbits in hiding, fearful of play,
Bats upside down hanging from eaves,
Oak trees adorning acorn and leaves.
Whispering grass, musky and sweet
Fragrance of bluebells, odour of peat.
Strange little sounds, buzzing of bees,
Shimmering leaves, gold from the trees,
Butterflies flutter in two, admiral red
Landing on lilac fly over your head
Primroses pretty scattered in clumps.
Midges that bite, giving you bumps
In the evening of sunset close of the day,
A wise owl that hoots has nothing to say,
Peaceful and tranquil now ebbing away,
Wonderful sights to end a fine day.

Nights of Silence

I had a dream that peace was here;
No more bombs, guns and fear,
Nights of silence and quiet sleep,
No more anguished mums who weep.
I had a dream that it would last,
No more heartbreak from the past,
No sons and dads left to bleed,
Laid in ground turned to weed.
Nights of silence, shattered dreams;
Reality is all it seems.
To turn it back so many years,
Bringing back so many fears.
This dream I had, it did not last,
Ugly heads rear from the past,
Nights of silence, oh no more
The pain, is back just like before,
And oh for why what reason, why
Do our loved ones have to die?
The child with oh such pleading eyes
Clasps mummy's hands as she cries,
And oh this dream, a nightmare now.
Nights of silence gone somehow,
But we must pray that peace will come
For me, for you, for everyone.

Clothe Me In Light

Lady of the night, clothe me in light,
Wrap up my shadows so that I might
Cast them away at the end of the day.
Silhouette lost in my shadow has given
Comfort to my soul with the stillness of night.
Wake up my spirit to help me to fight
All that has anguished my tired weary soul,
To help me attain my dream my goal.
If I had a choice when dawn has awoke
My weary old heart the task I revoke
I would have chosen a life that is free;
Away from all the hustle and bustle I see.
But then I would not have gained the wisdom
I've got the friends that I have, although I have some I've
    forgotten,
There's no point in changing my life of recluse,
My life's all arranged – but that's no excuse;
I've accepted it all as a matter of course
Things are not bad, they could have been worse.
I've lived life by choice, aware of the wonder of its source.

Snowdrop

As I raise my little head
Held by stems beneath this bed,
Seeing light, the very first,
Pushing up, out I burst.
I feel warmth, oh something wet,
Am I really ready yet?
To face this world, oh so big;
The rain, the snow. The gardeners dig
To pick me up and throw me down
With other weeds that lie around,
But if I make myself so white
Then go back in late at night,
For stronger I will grow each day
Until I'm big in every way,
Standing proudly in the soil.
It's not been easy, but heavy toil,
To push my way up to the top.
Sunflowers passing, they won't stop,
They have their beautiful height, looking down on me,
So small, so wee, a white snowdrop.

Wasted Years

Lost in the shadow of my frame
Helpless, alone, without a name.
In gambling everything I had I
Took my chances; times were bad.
Eternal youth is everlasting
Like a ship on a lost horizon
Sinking slowly without its masting
Yet hanging on to hope that comes
Over me in constant tidal waves,
I will see a ripple of the same
In this sea of vast despair,
Floating aimlessly in silence there
Wondering how to change my ways,
Make amends for useless wasted days.
In vain I clutch at broken straws,
Seeing every crack within my life.
All its meaning, all its flaws.
My soul is lost in blackened deep;
I've gambled at my own dear cost,
So now in anguished folly weep.
It is a waste of life, it's true,
But gambling, this disease I have,
Creeps up slowly then swallows you.
Chances are nothing has been ever gained

Except my broken heart and soul now stained.
I wait for solace in my hour of empathy;
It did not come for no one has any sympathy.

Sands and Horizons

I've walked on soft and sandy beach
Horizons there are out of reach;
Blue skies shrouded in sharpened clouds.
In peaceful calm, no maddening crowds
Warm sand nestles between your toes,
Tide that has its highs and lows.
Sun that kisses fair soft skin,
Fresh sea air breathed within.
Bracing winds tug at your hair,
Seagulls flying low
Steal a morsel from your hand
Return to young on cliffs and land.
Children with their castles built,
Screech with laughter, have no guilt
In knocking down all man-made towers
In sculptured sand and patient hours,
Made with so much love and want
By mothers, fathers or favourite aunts.
Waterlogged and washed away,
Have no choice how long they stay.
Setting sun low in the sky,
Rushing home, must say goodbye.
Tomorrow is another day
For resting, sleeping, time to play.

Seasons

Sweet breeze blow gently on my skin,
Calm the fears that lie within.
Gentle rain wash away my tears,
Strong winds blow away my fears.
Warm sun kissing on furrowed brow,
Snowflakes cold and soft somehow
Melt in haste, no time to stay,
Freeze in solid form, do not delay.
Seasons come and seasons go to waste,
God's gifts gone unnoticed because of haste
Amble if you can, for just one may
See God's creations every single way.
Be thankful for your blessings, always say
I thank you God for every single day.

Reclusive Mind

Standing still in the shadows
Of dusk's evening light
Moving now, hastily hidden
By the darkness of the night.
Fearless creature that I am,
Alone, the world no part of me.
Ambling time has now stood still,
I wait patiently, relentlessly, at will,
There is solitude in my heart to fulfil
An ambition of a different kind.
Reclused, the only solitude I can find,
Plentiful are the hours of the day
In easy peace which pass the time away,
Shrouded in blankets of silent hills,
Negative in my thoughts that fills
Me with such wonder and quiet calm.
No hustle, bustle or worried qualm;
I have not sought excitement, only peace.
My life is borrowed only out on lease,
The hours and days that I but own
Strangely, though, I never feel alone.

Eyes of a Child

I remember as clear as yesterday,
When on your knee I sat,
Your face so warm and smiling
And on your head a hat.
Your voice so sweet and gentle
The songs that you did sing
Of happenings so long ago.
The memories they evoked made
Your eyes so blue and misty.
This feeling of great woe;
I didn't want to leave you,
Yet hoping you would know
Even when a tear fell down
From the corner of your eye
I couldn't hug or comfort you
Say mummy please don't cry,
Today I still remember then.
It is vivid in my mind;
Knowing here that deep inside
Will I find someone so kind?
So now I've taught my children
The songs you sang to me,
And down the generations,
The same will always be

To keep our memories of you,
Your voice, your songs, that hat.
Oh, mother dear, I loved you.
I will always remember that.

When Jesus Called

Jesus, I am really well –
I trust in you and want to tell you
I still love you with all my heart.
I'd love to talk.
The late evenings draw so near,
I know that you are present here.
Take my hand, don't let it go,
With you I'll walk
Then there along the way,
As the sunset closes day,
Somehow I felt your kiss upon my brow,
Like the moonlight that you spill
On my pillow, soft and still.
With your help I'll get along, I know, somehow.
Yes, I know your tears are rain
When you dried them once again
You whisper to me in the trees and flowers,
For when the birds do sing
You gave me everything and are still by my side,
Watching over me for hours.
If sunshine is my clothes, your love indeed it shows
Is bigger than any want or need I yearn.
It's only then that I will know that you
    still love me so.

I'm not worthy of it all as yet but earned
Of the gifts that you have given
For the soul you tried to save,
It's only that you called to free me from sin
So when you knock upon my door,
I won't close it any more;
I'll make you welcome, take your hand
And let you in.

Spirits High and Low

When my spirit is low
It is helped by my weakness.
When my spirit is high,
It is lowered by my meekness.
If I am to inherit the earth,
Would my worldly goods be worth
Enough alone for me to carry on
The burdens that I have to shoulder?
Yet I am strong, wise, solid as a boulder,
To gain an inner strength of rock,
So to open every door to them who knock.
I will let them in through my heart alone,
For it is good and kind full of sweet atone.
If I can ease your pain for just one day.
Make you smile then wipe your tears away,
It's. this gift alone I share with troubled hearts,
So take it in your arms, your life now starts.

No Bed of Roses

Life has not been a bed of roses
Full of decisions and urgent disposes,
In order to live my live to the full
Impulsive in choice, regrets in a lull,
Sometimes I'd make a foolish mistake
Regretted so much it would keep me awake.
Arise in the morning, dreading the day
Aware of its warning, yet do as I may,
Hasty I might be in everyday things,
Slow in accepting the havoc it brings,
But I made my bed, in it, will I sleep.
It's not made of roses, weeds need to weep.
I scatter my seeds, hoping I've sowed
A plant made of money for debt that I owed.
All that is left is a hybrid or two,
One of them me, the other one you.
I've planted my roots and here I will stay,
I'm now down to earth to the end of the day,
Someday I'll grow up to be healthy and wise,
Meanwhile I'll hide in my bed of demise.

Memories and Daydreams

Lost in the past of memories sweet,
Silent in my thoughts buried deep,
Daydreams only last the time allowed,
Promises broken yet always vowed.
If my daydreams of you last for just one day,
Memories strong and vivid not to fade away,
I see your face in sorrow saddened,
Those tears still in your eyes
For the time that we did borrow,
I can hear your whispered sighs
Each memory that I hold so clear
They bring you close to me, so near,
And always you will be with me.
Memories help me find a way to see
That you are not that far away
With memories you are here to stay.

The Beggar

He stands there lonely in the street.
People pass him by,
Pretending not to see him
From the corner of their eye,
His hand held out in sadness,
He doesn't say let live,
Like he's become as invisible
As the money they don't give.
Sometimes you'll hear a jingle
From a person that has been kind,
Or a rustle of some paper
From someone with a compassionate mind.
This saddened sight before me,
Face hardened by his woe,
His frame become a shadow
This man we do not know.
But then again we shun him,
This beggar in the street,
With coat so torn and so forlorn
And no shoes upon his feet.
So be thankful for your blessings,
Be grateful for what you've got,
And never pass a beggar by,
Thank God that you are not.

Face of an Angel

Angels' faces, soft and wistful eyes,
Voices sweet and gentle whispered sighs.
Silken skin ivory without flaw –
You take my breath away
Whilst holding me in wondrous awe.
Your presence fills the empty room
With lightness in a darkened tomb.
Sylphlike is your shadowed frame,
Angelic like your chosen name
Created like a white and peaceful dove,
Loving, caring angel full of love,
Serene and graceful, loving, kind,
A species that is hard to find.
With golden hair and perfect wings
Fly away oh little one that sings,
Do not delay or miss what heaven brings,
Regal there adorned 'midst the Father of all kings.

The Vagabond

A vagabond I am but would you understand
As to why I take my thrift to such great lengths?
It was not because of greed I've got everything I need,
Gaining wisdom on my way from others' strengths
For what I do without as I freely roam about,
Enjoying life and all it has to give
For my pockets not weighed down by a shilling or a crown.
I get by, not having riches, the way I live.
Do I ever get depressed that I am poorly dressed?
It's my choice – I had to make it and I will strive
In that great big world out there, I haven't got a care
Of what or who I am or where I'll die,
So don't look down on me I've fooled you can't you see,
As you lay me in a grave without a name,
For I saved along the way, it's called a rainy day.
Strangely though the rain, it never came,
Yet in that great big world out there,
In my judgement were unfair. Did you clothe me,
Keep me warm or even care? It's a strange old world, alas,
For this vagabond you pass with no money is now a
    millionaire.

Out on a Wing

Oh, how I wish I could be
A bird, flying out on a wing,
To learn, to know, to see.
Yes indeed what life might bring
If I could fly beyond horizons new,
View them from a distance, change a few,
Then stretch my wings, see how things have changed
So much from in the past. Each spring so warm, cold
    winters
Left its wrath of barren trees, the wind, black frost that
No one sees yet feathered friend I am ruffled. That variety
Is the spice of life for humans, anyway, to be precise,
I will return if only just to see, perhaps you will remember
Me and in your trees of green, brown and gold
The flowers, nectar, bees still buzzing, fold their
    honeycomb
In soft layers, hold knowing that I have returned to nest,
To rear my young weary traveller, that I am I have to rest
Until I yearn to fly out on a wing again to find that when I
Return nothing has changed that much but yet will never
    be the same
Again.

Where Angels Go To Sleep

I could not say goodnight to you
That night there as you slept.
I never said goodbye to you
For all day I had wept.
Someone came and took you
From my tender loving care,
You drifted off so gently,
He said you're needed there.
I heard your little voice
As you did leave me then,
An angel came to tell me
The time, the place, and when.
I couldn't take away your pain
Your suffering was too much.
This angel then he said to me,
God needed you as such.
You left me like a whisper
In the stillness of the night,
For as you gently flew away
I saw a shining light.
It was so bright it blinded me
Yet someone I could see,
An angel looking down at me
He said you'd be all right.

I felt your hand caress my face
Then kiss my brow so sweet,
To tell me that you're happy now,
And somewhere we will meet.
I know your in a better place
Where angels go to sleep.
I let you go because I know
That angels do not weep.
So watch over me I will be
Content for just one day
But promise me tomorrow send
An angel past this way.
I'll take his hand to take a peep
My broken heart will mend
To join you there, come what may
Where angels go to sleep.

Time Does Not Wait

It's true to say that time must not be lost
Though often it can always slip away at cost.
Priceless it may be, it's there, it's going free,
Yet wasted in a moment, slipped away from you and me
The years are counted, birthdays come and go
In scores, then in decades are we ashamed that this is so,
But we can't hold back the years or the hands of father time.
Of course we can't, we age like good wine;
Matured is what we are, like a good old vintage car.
Wiser than an owl but he is older yet by far,
Yet had we spread our wings, done many different things,
Would we regret the time we lost and everything it brings?
Time is like a cup you must fill and use it up – do not waste.
What God has given to you each day, never use it up with haste,
For He has not got so much time to let it slip away,
So use your time up wisely, it will come as no surprise
That tomorrow will come and bring a brand new day.

Wasting Time

I have no time to stop and stare,
My life is filled with haste.
To take the time to be aware
For some this time they waste.
It's only when that time goes by
That they wonder where? Yet asking why,
They say how much that time did fly
For they didn't have the time
To see a time when life was great.
Some other time, you couldn't wait
For time to pass, maybe too late,
Because they didn't take the time.
If you are one of these above
You've missed the time to share to love,
To watch, to listen, time to see.
It's there to use and time is free,
Regret in time that you have not
For the time you lost now haven't got.
So take the time of essence fast,
Use it. up but make it last.
To keep your life together now
For time that you have lost somehow.

Selfish Ambition

I had great ambitions clearly in my mind,
Striving, climbing, solving problems of every kind.
Determination in order to reach my avid goal,
Relentless and sometimes selfish, burning in my soul
Getting to the top of a mountain, black and white,
Falling into black holes when ambition lost its sight,
Yet ruthless in my goals in a way that I must win.
Not a thought of others or predicaments they were in.
Perhaps my selfish ways were looked upon with shame;
I had to earn a living, yet get rich easy was my aim.
I used a lot of people on my way right to the top;
Others' feelings didn't matter, in fact, I couldn't stop
As the buzz that it gave me meant I really didn't care
About my fellow peers or indeed of anyone out there.
It was only when my health went down that I couldn't take the pace.
I realised that out there was a different kind of race;
Those that I had treated with contempt and no remorse,
Used them all along the way, sometimes with no recourse
But I have changed since finding these people salt of the earth who
Have helped me through my sickness, yet made me feel of worth.
My friends I have are blessings now as I'm in failing health
They stood by me and gave it free, regardless of my wealth.

Meadows Soft and Green

In the meadows so sweet, soft and green,
Such wonderful sights that I've seen;
The dancing of grass to and fro,
Wide open spaces with nowhere to go
Daffodils, daisies a bluebell or two,
The buzz of the bee is music to you.
In your mind you can picture it all
The joy from a bird in some mating call
From an oak tree. You cannot revoke
The rabbit, the hare, that sat staring there,
Then ran past me just as I spoke.
Butterflies flutter into colours and pairs,
Even old scarecrow in old tattered wares
Shows a look of surprise and raises his eyes
when a bird lands on him in sense of his guise
Then flies away, out on a wing.
I'm really sure that I heard him sing
A song oh, so sweet in some form of greeting
In getting away from old scarecrow that day,
Maybe tomorrow will be different I'd say,
Yet tranquil beauty is all that I see,
Like peace and contentment a feeling so free,
As I stand in the meadows so sweet, soft and green,
Thankful I have stood here and for all that I've seen.

In Memories of Sleep

Lost in a world, silent and deep,
Trying to find the secret of peaceful sleep.
What solace do I find to ease my weary head,
Sensitive to a deed or something that's been said,
Then to touch my soul with feelings of such hate
To change my life, my destiny, possibly my fate.
I do not wish to flee but fight.
But sleep will not be mine. I wait.
The hours so long in this lonely night,
I lie awake to greet the early morn,
Lack of sleep, listless sad so forlorn
I greet the day tired and with wearied soul,
Not reaching any dream or avid goal,
Only acceptance of another day to fill,
Where time, it seems to me, is standing still.
Yet heartened by the nature of the day,
The sun and April showers, amidst this may
I linger with my thoughts, the passing years,
Moments that I laughed, cried away my tears,
Washed away in silence, down the many years.

Gifts of Love

Love is like an ocean, wider than the sea,
Given out at any time, love is always free.
If you have this special gift, treasure it alone,
Use it well and cast its spell in every wanting home.
Send it out in bouquets of lovely perfumed flowers.
Show it in a kiss or two if absent for some hours,
Feel it in your heart when someone else is low,
Enfold them with your arms of love, never let them go.
Listen to a friend who's down, they will need it then.
Let them know that you are there to share it all with them.
Love is for eternity, it should last for many years,
Share it, show it, give it out to banish others' tears.
Lasting love is everything, without it you can't live,
Hold it, keep it, save it up in order just to give
Someone with a broken heart, a reason to go on,
Knowing that you've done your part in loving for so long.
Finally a special love, the one you feel for me.
I sent it down for you to use in a parcel that is free.
I hadn't time to wrap it up in fancy little bows,
It makes no difference how it's wrapped, only if it shows.

Creations

Clothe me in warm sunshine,
Spill moonlight on my face,
Make my tears the rain again
So they vanish without trace.
Whisper in the soft green grass
In the colours of the flowers,
Let the birds sing love songs
Yet watch over me for hours.
A warm breeze just to rest me
When the sunset it does close,
Then kiss my brow so softly now
Like the petals from a rose.
The leaves and trees have whispered
There's stillness in the air,
I know you're here beside me,
Right here I feel, but where?
So take my hand and lead me
For I am blind not free,
And let your hands now guide you
To the land where I can see.

Days and Dreams Gone By

I had seen better days when dreams had gone by,
Days that were happy, days when I'd cry.
Dreams, some were broken, others came true
In some form of token from out of the blue.
The times that I'd dream about wonderful things
The days that I'd do what life always brings.
I don't feel I've wasted these fifty loaned years;
I've felt and I've tasted my joys and my tears.
I'm poor and so wise, yet rich in my health.
My days and my dreams are in enriched without wealth
For I would not change the days that I had,
The dreams that I wasted, the times that were bad,
Days that have gone but I don't question why.
Beautiful dreams in days have gone by,
It's made me much wiser, so gentle and kind,
Knowing they're deep and locked up in my mind.

The Gambler

You see him there, a lonely figure,
Although it doesn't show,
In his heart there is a secret
Not wishing you to know
In his mind there's desperation,
Cold sweat upon his brow.
In a catch-22 situation,
To win it back somehow,
But in silence he is trying,
He will try and try again,
For time that he is buying
Again it's all in vain.
His family life is shattered
With dignity that's all gone,
As nothing else had mattered:
It just went on and on.
But pity him, this creature,
It's an illness, that's the truth,
In gambling away his future
Alas he has lost his youth.

Deep Rivers, High Mountains

Lost in the depth of an ocean
Surrounded by mountains so high,
My mind is aloft in slow motion.
This heart in a permanent sigh,
My feelings are silent, skin deep,
Hidden by sad eyes that weep,
Alone with my thoughts of despair.
The world of society out there,
Oblivious without any feeling or care
Of others' misfortune, despair and ill health.
Life's too important, enjoying their wealth,
Selfish it seems but that's what life brings;
A world of reality, like a bird with no wings.
Helpless they be between heaven and earth,
It's now plain to see that money is greed.
Unaware of the fact there are others in need,
But they have the best of two different goals.
Not filled with illusion or black indulged holes,
For they wouldn't change the wisdom they've gained
For the sun in their lives, for each time it rained,
Some pennies from heaven, yet grateful they've got
A life that's so humble, while others have not.

Simplicity of Life

I have no political point of view,
Those that have, I've no objections to.
If my choice offends it's mine alone,
For only God will judge my life and atone.
Simplicity in life is all I wish to seek,
For He has promised me the earth
If I am gentle and I meek,
But that will come when I am dead
With daisies right above my head;
That's the solace that I seek,
To be forgotten whilst I lie
In a cemetery of lasting peace.
Don't cry for me, wipe your eyes,
Your tears, they have to cease.
Use your tears to wash away
Another person's sin.
Save them for another day,
Keep them held within.
Don't cry for me, I cannot stay
There's some things you never win.

Angels from Above

When God made angels from above,
He made them gentle, filled with love
Cherubs spiritual, soft and sweet,
With wistful eyes and little feet,
Laughing faces with fairy wings,
Loving, giving voice that sings,
Serene and peaceful cherub face,
Silk and woven, white as lace,
Evening brings a peaceful ending
To my mind, my heart that is mending,
My spirits lifted held aloft
By angels flying gently soft,
Whispers touch my furrowed brow,
Stay there sweetly, gentle now.
Quiet sleep I had last night,
Restful, tranquil a shining light
Calms my fears for evermore
Shrouded by your mantle wore,
For you came in and took my pain
Then gave me back my life again.
You gave it back in scented flowers,
I now can see the time, the hours
Every day is fresh and bright,
Bringing forth an angel's light

To shine upon my soul that's led
Where wise men fear to go alone,
Yet you did not fear to tread.

The Coming of Spring

You can almost feel it in the air,
Birds singing, buzzing bees out there,
Nestling young in the trees and eaves,
Buds bursting open, turning into leaves.
Snowdrops pretty small and soft, snow white,
Hiding, peeping in their beds at night,
Pushing forth up at the sun's first light,
Daffodils yellow – what a pretty sight!
Morning's green grass wet with dew
Seen by only some, a chosen few
Who may arise to greet the spring
To see what wondrous beauty it does bring.
Butterflies with colours, oh so bright,
Caught in sunshine rapturous light.
Cabbage white peacock and admiral red
Cuckoos lazy in a nest have laid
A claim to other homes of nesting young
Before the dawn and chorus ritual song.
Amble slowly on an April sunny day and you may
Take in the wonders there in many ways.
Do we take the time to see this beauty going free?
Babbling brooks and rippled frogspawned streams,
Meadows plush and filled with daisies, mellow greens.
Even squirrels have been seen, a species oh so rare,

Is that a rabbit or a hare in a burrow over there?
Spring we know is not that very long a special thing,
If you have heard the cuckoos song bring a melody,
Miss it not when it does call or sing to you or me;
It's telling you of the coming days of spring.

Blood Really Counts

I had a dream that everything
Was peaceful in our land.
No mothers' tears and children's fears,
They who will never understand
Why some can take away a life
With no feelings of remorse,
Take a father from a wife,
Give religion as a reason.
Are we not in Christian days?
Your neighbour you should love
Does it matter where he prays?
It's not questioned from above
For you have been created
By the Maker that's the same.
In some ways, we're related,
Yet you do not know my name.
I've asked my sole creator
To send me down some blood,
It's needed now not later –
I'd buy it if I could.
It isn't labelled with a name,
Whose religion it is from,
Yet badly needed all the same,
For me, for you, for some,

So think before you take a life,
One day before too long
His blood group might save your child or wife –
It's then you'll know it's wrong to fight.

Peace in our Green and Pleasant Land

When will we have peace in our
Green and pleasant land?
Why won't sense prevail on them?
Will they never understand
That our children are our future?
What example do they show
To kill to maim to mutilate
The innocent that we know,
Are we not that civilised?
God said thou shalt not kill.
His commandments now are broken,
The sixth one just at will.
How can they sleep in bed at night
When their Maker they shall meet?
For heaven is a nicer place
But hell is full of heat.
He's judging at the present now
A verdict He has reached.
You didn't listen to His Word
Or practise what He preached.
A judgement from the man above
Is thorough and very fair,
He knows exactly what you've done,
The time, the place, and where.

Compassion is not in His heart
Did you have it then?
For families that you tore apart,
Fathers and young men,
Don't waste His time. He's had enough.
His patience running thin,
Don't knock the gates of heaven's door
But hell takes those who sin,
So Christian be in what you do
To enter heaven's gates
For your Maker He is watching,
He judges your life, your fates.

Mechanical Inventions

What is the point in mechanical inventions?
I'm sure they are made with all good intentions
Phones that will tell if you're out or you're in,
Washers that wash and dryers that spin.
Contraptions that change the whole human race
With switches and buttons all over the place.
Gone are the days when we would sit and talk,
Now they have cars, with no time to walk.
I'm all for progression, that's got to be done,
But not for inventions. They're all right for some but
The pace is so fast that I cannot keep track.
Why can't I cope, is there something I lack?
It's not that I'm missing a brain cell or two,
But my common sense tells me as to what I should do.
I don't need any buttons to get me to play,
Or lights that will tell me to go the right way.
The alarm in my head tells me when to get up,
My stomach's my clock that tells I need to sup.
These legs are my wheels, they never wear out,
This voice box my music when I have to shout,
I know that you're thinking I'm decrepit and old,
But don't be so sure as my life's not on hold.

I can replay all my actions and stop them you see;
For there's one thing I'm sure of and always will be
I don't need electric to move or run me.

Autumn Leaves

Trees stand there stark and lonely,
Stretching out towards the sky.
If you take the time to listen
You can almost hear them sigh.
For when their last grips dawning
And time for leaves to fall
On a cold and windy morning
Their bearers no more pall,
Yet as they gently flutter
Falling wistful to the ground,
You hear whispers: are they sighing?
Then eerie silence all around
The silhouette of nature's cold
Strips father oak a king of old
Leaving strewn around great colours,
Some green and rust and gold.

Sarcasm and Wit

Sarcasm is the lowest form of wit,
Uttered when your wit is low.
It's not the wit that's uttered
But just how far you'll go
To bring a person's spirit down
To make them feel very small.
So what's the point in slagging
Or saying anything at all
To hurt someone badly?
It doesn't mean you're smart
Or even very clever
To break somebody's heart.
So think before you utter
Some sarcastic words of wit,
You might become the wearer of
The cap that doesn't fit.
It's nothing to be proud of,
So hold your head in shame,
At least I've got my pride intact
And most of all my name.

Inspirations

I wish that I could be inspired
By things I haven't done,
And no regrets about the past
Or battles that I've won.
If inspiration's the only thing
To really be inspired,
Then why am I unhappy?
When I've everything desired.
Perhaps it was and just because
It was handed on a plate
I got it all so easily
Sooner rather than late.
But the more I have the more I want,
I'm not happy with my lot.
But wealth becomes a mystery
When health I haven't got.
Well now that I've decided
That money is not wealth
And most of all important
It doesn't buy your health,
I'm starting to be sensible
Since becoming really wise,
I've now got health and dignity
Not things that I despise.

The Wanderer

I had a wandering lust
That lay deep within my soul,
Travelling was my forte.
Before my spirit would grow old
I packed my bags and started
Off on a cold and winter's day,
Not looking back and in my sack
A map to show my way.
It was a kind of freedom
That's not easy to explain,
The reason for my wandering
Kept running through my veins.
No fear did overcome me
As I travelled here and there,
No time to age, feel any rage,
I was always free from care.
Then one day came this feeling
Of wandering felt no more;
It did not feel so urgent,
Not like it did before.
It was strangely on my travels
Where I met this lovely lass,
Rich, so young and beautiful
I travel now first class.

Stolen Jewel

You have been stolen from us
By a King amongst kings
To be an ambassador in heaven
With angels that sing.
There are no pictures or parasites
Destroying your soul; you are with the Father of all
Who's now sharing your goals,
Worthy you are of your final place.
At peace like an angel in glory and grace
Sleep in the knowledge so worthy of peace
Aware that the cameras and clicking have ceased.
Laugh with the angels, try out your wings,
Enjoy every moment that every day brings.
Our loss is God's gain, but we will never forget
Your infinite beauty, the people you met.
A star now in heaven with God by your side
For I have been told He was waiting outside
To welcome you home at those white pearly gates,
In the hope that an angel passes by as He waits.

Princess in Heaven

You were the princess of them all,
Regardless of all protocol
An angel of mercy, Queen of all hearts,
Your life has not ended, it's now that it starts.
Somebody stole you for just a short time,
It was God that has told me, says now she in mine.
I needed an angel to help me up here,
I chose her because of her passion so dear.
Now she is sleeping in peace by my side,
I made her most welcome, with my arms open wide.
I will not awake her as she needs to rest.
Her job starts tomorrow for today she's my guest.
The picture you want, I cannot send down
By now you have guessed there's no camera around.
But now she's in heaven with a crown on her head
One that is regal for the life that she lead.
Down at her feet is one single rose red
For William and Harry, what more can be said?